P
597.98
Gal

ZOO ANIMALS

Alligators and Crocodiles

Debbie Gallagher

Marshall Cavendish
Benchmark
New York

This edition first published in 2010 in the United States of America by Marshall Cavendish Benchmark
An imprint of Marshall Cavendish Corporation

All rights reserved.

No part of this publication may be reproduced, stored in a retrieval system or transmitted, in any form or by any means, electronic, mechanical, photocopying, recording, or otherwise, without the prior permission of the copyright owner. Request for permission should be addressed to the Publisher, Marshall Cavendish Corporation, 99 White Plains Road, Tarrytown, NY 10591. Tel: (914) 332-8888, fax: (914) 332-1888.

Website: www.marshallcavendish.us

This publication represents the opinions and views of the author based on Debbie Gallagher's personal experience, knowledge, and research. The information in this book serves as a general guide only. The author and publisher have used their best efforts in preparing this book and disclaim liability rising directly and indirectly from the use and application of this book.

Other Marshall Cavendish Offices:
Marshall Cavendish Ltd. 5th Floor, 32-38 Saffron Hill, London EC1N 8FH, UK • Marshall Cavendish International (Asia) Private Limited, 1 New Industrial Road, Singapore 536196 • Marshall Cavendish International (Thailand) Co Ltd. 253 Asoke, 12th Flr, Sukhumvit 21 Road, Klongtoey Nua, Wattana, Bangkok 10110, Thailand • Marshall Cavendish (Malaysia) Sdn Bhd, Times Subang, Lot 46, Subang Hi-Tech Industrial Park, Batu Tiga, 40000 Shah Alam, Selangor Darul Ehsan, Malaysia

Marshall Cavendish is a trademark of Times Publishing Limited

All websites were available and accurate when this book was sent to press.

Library of Congress Cataloging-in-Publication Data

Gallagher, Debbie, 1969-
    Alligators and crocodiles / Debbie Gallagher. — 1st ed.
       p. cm. — (Zoo animals)
    Includes index.
    Summary: "Discusses alligators and crocodiles, their natural habitat, behavior, characteristics, and zoo life"—Provided by publisher.
    ISBN 978-0-7614-4743-6
    1. Alligators—Juvenile literature. 2. Crocodiles—Juvenile literature.
    I. Title.
    SF408.6.A54G35 2010
    639.3'98—dc22
                                                          2009039864

3 5944 00113 1547

First published in 2010 by
MACMILLAN EDUCATION AUSTRALIA PTY LTD
15–19 Claremont Street, South Yarra 3141

Visit our website at www.macmillan.com.au or go directly to www.macmillanlibrary.com.au

Associated companies and representatives throughout the world.

Copyright © Debbie Gallagher 2010

Edited by Georgina Garner
Text and cover design by Kerri Wilson
Page layout by Raul Diche
Photo research by Legend Images
Base maps by Gaston Vanzet, modified by Kerri Wilson

Printed in the United States

Acknowledgments
The author and the publisher are grateful to the following for permission to reproduce copyright material:

Front cover photo of Nile crocodiles in Kenya courtesy of Photolibrary/Michael Krabs

Photographs courtesy of: © PCL/Alamy, **29**; Bristol Zoo Gardens, **22**; Matthew Field, **7**; © Clark Wheeler/iStockphoto, **3**; © Linda Waterhouse/iStockphoto, **11**; Legendimages, **4**, **20**; Paignton Zoo Environmental Park, **13**, **14**, **16**, **17**, **21**, **24**, **25**; Photolibrary © BRUCE COLEMAN INC./Alamy, **28**; Photolibrary © Ron Buskirk/Alamy, **26** (right); Photolibrary © imagebroker/Alamy, **27** (right); Photolibrary/Mark Deeble & Victoria Stone, **18**; Photolibrary/Aaron Ferster, **12**; Photolibrary/Harold W Hoffman, **19**; Photolibrary/Michael Krabs, **1**; Photolibrary/Photo Researchers, **10**; © Potapov Alexander/Shutterstock, **8** (silhouettes); © beltsazar/Shutterstock, **5**; © Joyce Mar/Shutterstock, **6**; © WCS, **27** (left), **30**; Julie Larsen Maher © WCS, **15**, **26** (left); Wikimedia Commons, photo by Adrian Pingstone, **23**.

Many zoos helped in the creation of this book. The authors would especially like to thank Paignton Zoo Environmental Park, England, ZooParc de Beauval, France, Wildlife Conservation Society, Bronx Zoo, USA, and Bristol Zoo Gardens, England.

While every care has been taken to trace and acknowledge copyright, the publisher tenders their apologies for any accidental infringement where copyright has proved untraceable. Where the attempt has been unsuccessful, the publisher welcomes information that would redress the situation.

1 3 5 6 4 2

Contents

Zoos	4
Alligators and Crocodiles	6
In the Wild	8
Zoo Homes	12
Zoo Food	14
Zoo Health	16
Baby Alligators and Crocodiles	18
How Zoos Are Saving Alligators and Crocodiles	20
Meet Sam, a Crocodile Keeper	24
A Day in the Life of a Zookeeper	26
Zoos Around the World	28
The Importance of Zoos	30
Glossary	31
Index	32

When a word is printed in **bold**, you can look up its meaning in the Glossary on page 31.

Zoos

Zoos are places where people can see a lot of different animals. The animals in a zoo come from all around the world.

People can visit zoos to see animals from other parts of the world.

Zoos have special **enclosures** for different types of animals. Some enclosures are like the animals' homes in the **wild**. They may have trees for climbing or water for swimming.

Forest animals, such as gorillas, need enclosures filled with plants and trees.

Alligators and Crocodiles

Alligators and crocodiles are **reptiles**. They have short legs, strong tails, and long, powerful **jaws**. A crocodile has a longer and thinner **snout** than an alligator.

strong tail · eyes on top of head · short legs

webbed back feet · thick scales · short, wide snout

American alligators grow to about 13 feet (4 meters) long.

There are fourteen different **species** of crocodiles and two species of alligators. All have thick, scaly skin and bony plates along their backs and tails. Some have stripes or spots.

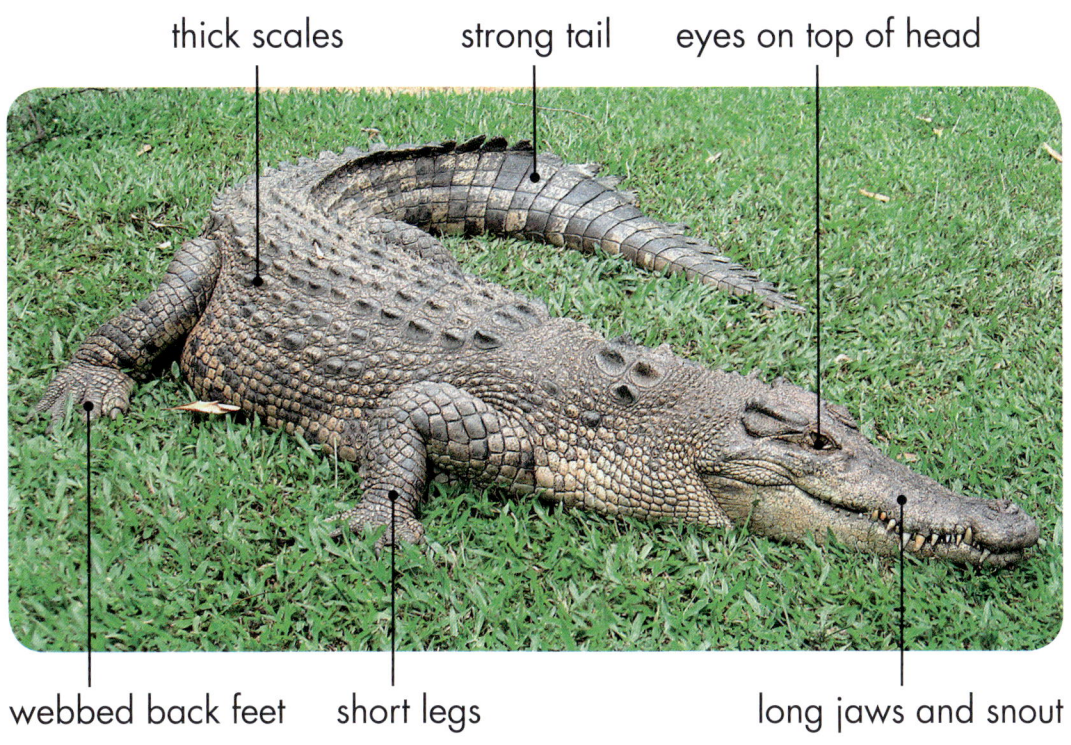

thick scales   strong tail   eyes on top of head

webbed back feet   short legs   long jaws and snout

Saltwater crocodiles are the biggest crocodiles and can grow up to 23 feet (7 m) long.

In the Wild

In the wild, alligators and crocodiles live in warm or hot areas. They often live on their own, but form groups to hunt and to raise their young.

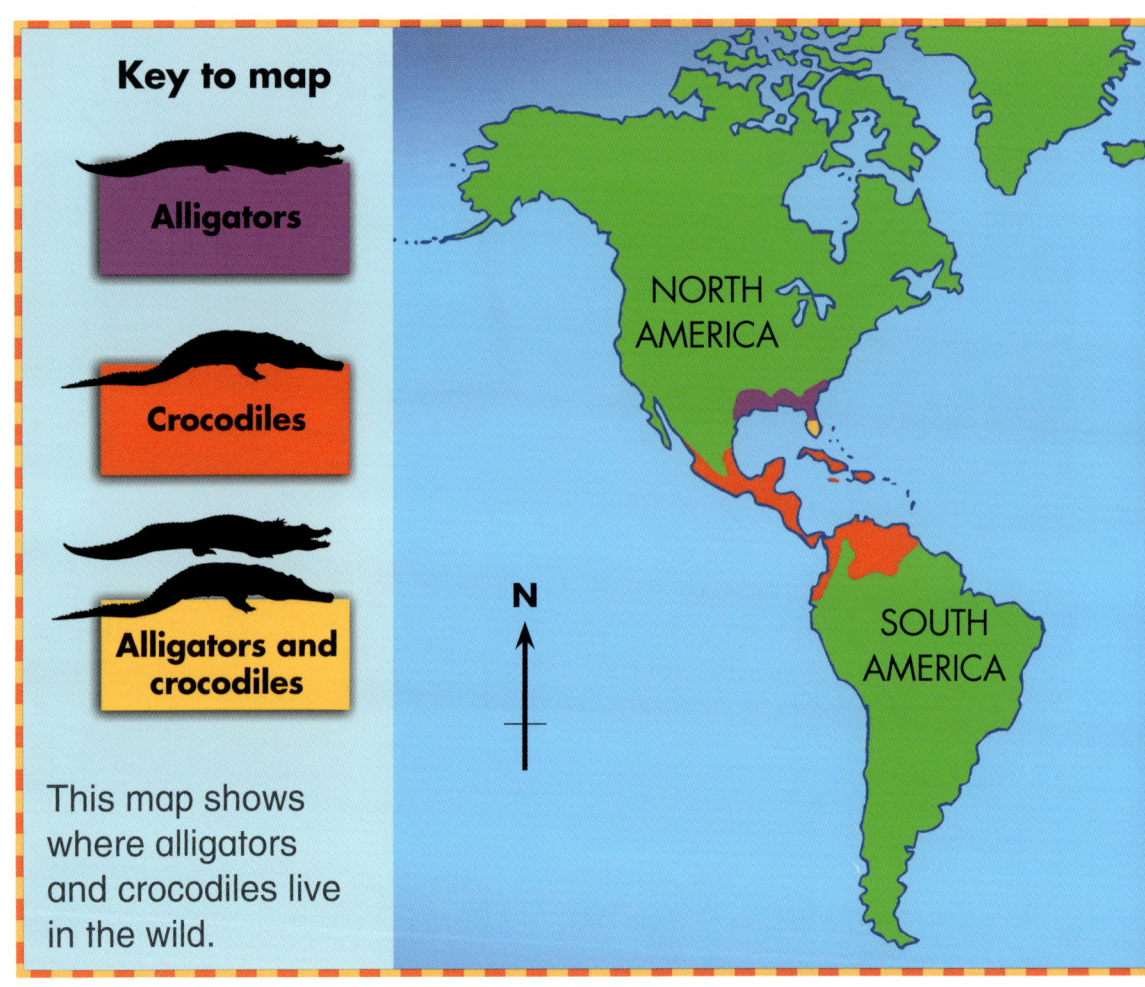

Key to map

Alligators

Crocodiles

Alligators and crocodiles

This map shows where alligators and crocodiles live in the wild.

Alligators and crocodiles live both in water and on the land. Crocodiles live in salt water or freshwater. Alligators prefer freshwater.

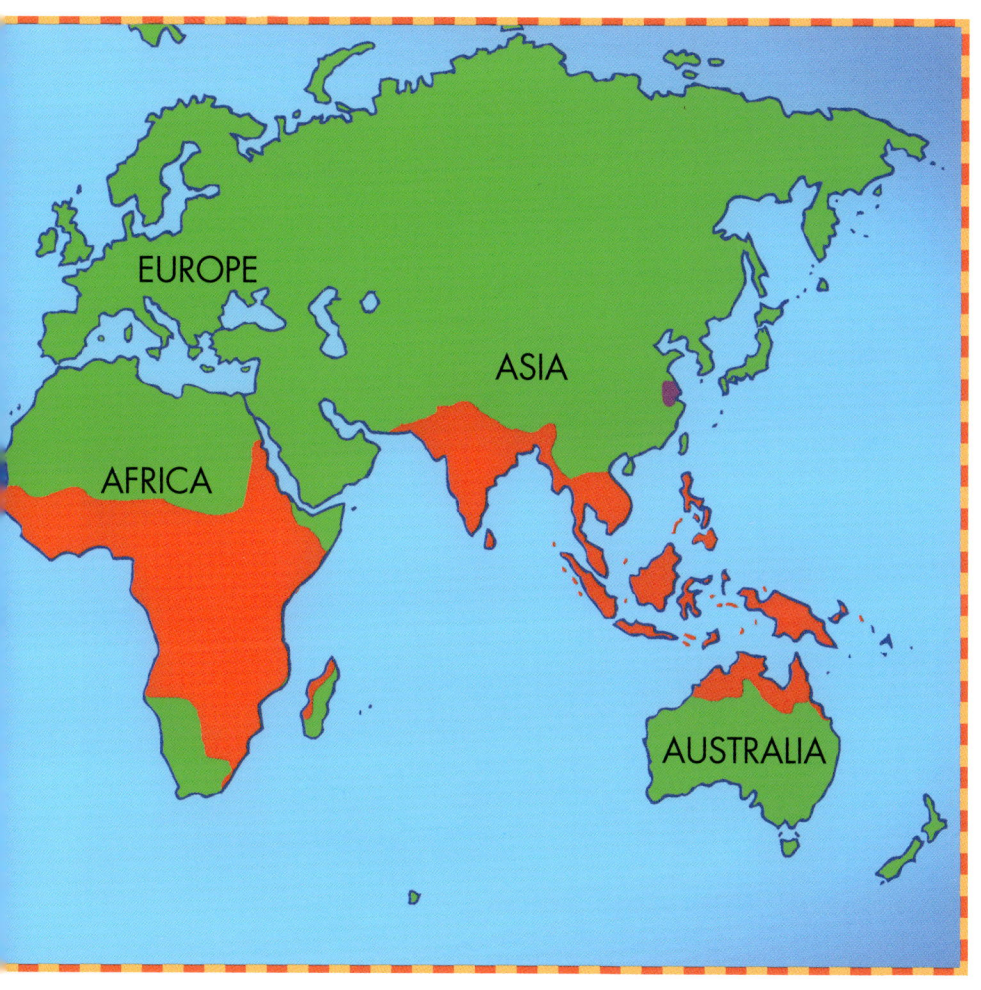

Threats to Survival

The biggest threat to alligators and crocodiles is the clearing of land. Their **habitats** are destroyed to make room for buildings and farms.

An American alligator lies by the water in its natural habitat.

Another threat is hunters who kill alligators and crocodiles for their **hides**. The hides are used to make boots, belts, and bags.

Hunters get paid a lot of money for the crocodile skins used to make handbags.

Zoo Homes

In zoos, alligators and crocodiles live in enclosures. These enclosures are built to be like their habitats in the wild. There are a lot of big plants and pools of water.

plants

pool of water

An alligator enclosure has areas of land and water.

The enclosures need to be warm because alligators and crocodiles come from warm areas. The air also needs to be damp.

plants

An enclosure is warm and damp like a crocodile's habitat in the wild.

Zoo Food

In zoos, alligators and crocodiles are fed dead animals, such as chickens. They eat all of the dead animal, including the bones. The bones help keep them healthy.

A zookeeper takes food to the alligators and crocodiles.

Zoo Food for Alligators and Crocodiles
whole chickens
whole rats
whole rabbits
fish
lumps of meat

Feeding

Alligators and crocodiles do not eat often. Zookeepers feed them once a week. The keepers use a pole to hold out the food or throw it into the enclosure.

A crocodile grabs a dead chicken from a zookeeper.

Zoo Health

Zookeepers look after the animals to make sure they stay healthy. The enclosure is cleaned every day. Grassy areas are mowed and the water in the ponds is cleaned.

A zookeeper checks the water temperature in the enclosure.

Zookeepers watch each of the alligators and crocodiles in the enclosure. They check that the animals are behaving normally. They make notes in a diary about anything unusual.

The zookeepers notice if an alligator or crocodile seems unhappy or sick.

Baby Alligators and Crocodiles

Alligators and crocodiles make nests for their eggs on land. The mother lays up to eighty eggs in her nest. All the eggs hatch at the same time.

Baby crocodiles hatch from their eggs.

Baby alligators and crocodiles, called hatchlings, stay with their mothers for up to one year. The mother and other adults look after them as they learn to swim and hunt.

A baby alligator suns itself on its mother's back.

How Zoos Are Saving Alligators and Crocodiles

Zoos often save alligators and crocodiles that are living close to humans. The animals are caught and taken to live in zoos. In a zoo, they are safe from hunters.

Alligators and crocodiles are protected in a zoo.

Some zoos have "Adopt-an-Alligator" programs. People donate money so that an alligator can receive proper care at the zoo. They are given a photograph of their "adopted" alligator and information about the animal.

Zoos raise money to save alligators when people "adopt" an alligator.

Zoos Working Together

Zoos work together by sharing animals. Bristol Zoo, in England, **breeds** West African dwarf crocodiles. It sends some of its baby crocodiles to other zoos.

Zoos work together and share baby West African dwarf crocodiles.

In Africa, local people hunt West African dwarf crocodiles for food and for hides. Sharing and breeding these crocodiles helps make sure they do not become **endangered**.

A West African dwarf crocodile is protected in its zoo enclosure.

Meet Sam, a Crocodile Keeper

Sam works as a zookeeper at the Paignton Zoo, in England.

Question How did you become a zookeeper?

Answer I studied **animal management**, and then applied for the job—simple!

Question How long have you been a zookeeper?

Answer I have been a zookeeper for two years.

Sam gets ready to feed the animals.

Question	What animals have you worked with?
Answer	I have worked with Nile crocodiles, Cuban crocodiles, saltwater crocodiles, pythons, and boa constrictors.
Question	What do you like about your job?
Answer	I like getting so close to such amazing animals!

A Day in the Life of a Zookeeper

Zookeepers have jobs they do every day. Often, a team of zookeepers work together to look after the reptiles at a zoo.

8:30 a.m.
Clean the crocodile and alligator enclosures.

12:00 p.m.
Meet with visitors and show them the baby alligators and crocodiles.

4:00 p.m.
Prepare meat for the animals.

5:00 p.m.
Feed chickens to the alligators.

Zoos Around the World

There are many different zoos around the world. Gatorland Zoo is in Florida. There are more than one thousand alligators and two hundred crocodiles at the zoo.

Visitors watch alligators from special boardwalks at Gatorland Zoo.

Gatorland is in the Florida Everglades, which is a natural habitat of American alligators. The zoo is covered in natural lakes and **marshes**.

Alligators lie on the banks of a marsh at Gatorland.

The Importance of Zoos

Zoos do very important work. They:
- help people learn about animals
- save endangered animals and animals that are badly treated

This endangered Chinese alligator was born in a zoo then placed in the wild.

Glossary

animal management	Looking after and dealing with animals.
breeds	Caring for animals so that they can produce babies.
enclosures	The fenced-in areas where animals are kept in zoos.
endangered	At high risk of dying out and disappearing from Earth.
habitats	Areas in which animals are naturally found.
hides	Animal skins.
jaws	The bones that form the mouth and hold the teeth.
marshes	Wet, grassy lands that sometimes flood.
reptiles	A group of animals, such as snakes and crocodiles, with dry, scaly skin.
snout	Nose and mouth area that sticks out of the face.
species	Groups of animals or plants that have similar features.
wild	Natural areas, such as forests, that are untouched by humans.

Index

a
American alligators, 6, 10, 29
animal health, 14, 16–17

b
baby animals, 18–19, 22, 22, 26
breeding, 22, 23
Bristol Zoo, 22

c
Chinese alligators, 30
Cuban crocodiles, 25

e
enclosures, 5, 12–13, 15, 16, 17
endangered animals, 23, 30

f
food, 14–15, 27

g
Gatorland Zoo, 28, 29

h
habitats, 10, 12, 29

hatchlings, 19
hides, 11, 23
hunters, 11, 20

l
land clearing, 10

n
nests, 18
Nile crocodiles, 25

p
Paignton Zoo, 24

s
saltwater crocodiles, 7, 25

t
threats to survival, 10–11

w
West African dwarf crocodiles, 22, 23
wild animals, 5, 8–9

z
zookeepers, 14, 15, 16, 17, 24–5, 26–7
zoo projects, 22–3

FEB - - 2010